JAN HEDGER first sta... her hometown of Birm... years living away in Ber... of Scotland. Leaving Birm... ...er poetry continued to flourish and de... ...working at Swindon College, where she receive... great deal of inspiration and encouragement. It was in this period where she gained an A* English GCSE at the mature age of 46! Jan's love of life and her interest in a wide range of subjects is reflected in her poetry. She has had sixteen poems previously published in anthologies and regularly performs her work. Jan believes poetry should be accessible to everyone. Her first book *Words in Imagination* was published in 2008.

Jan now lives in Bexhill on Sea, East Sussex, with her husband Nigel.

GARDENING LEAVE

£1 from the sale of this book goes to Gardening Leave
www.gardeningleave.org

Gardening Leave is a registered charity set up in 2007 to provide Horticultural Therapy for ex-Service personnel with combat-related mental health troubles.

The veterans who come to Gardening Leave mostly live alone, due to the mental health troubles which blight their lives; flashbacks, nightmares, intrusive thoughts and hyper vigilance. Being at Gardening Leave means they can spend time with other veterans who 'speak the same language', be outside, and have something semi-structured to do in safe, peaceful surroundings where our staff and volunteers will treat them with respect and understanding.

The Horticultural Therapy the veterans receive helps to reduce their social isolation by giving them back confidence, self-esteem, improved concentration and physical condition. It helps to divert them from the flashbacks and intrusive thoughts and encourages social interaction.

In our first year, 125 veterans received 703 half day sessions of Horticultural Therapy. In our second year, these figures increased to 342 veterans receiving 1,249 half day sessions. Over seventy percent chose to return to Gardening Leave and the structure, routine and exercise we offer.

GL relies entirely on voluntary contributions and we are extremely grateful to Jan for her generosity in including us in her book.

*Anna Baker Cresswell*
GARDENING LEAVE
Registered in England 6091057. Charity Number 1119786.
Charity Registered in Scotland SCO038563

Published in paperback by SilverWood Books 2010
www.silverwoodbooks.co.uk

Copyright © Jan Hedger 2010

The right of Jan Hedger to be identified as the author of this work
has been asserted by her in accordance with the Copyright,
Designs and Patents Act 1988.

All characters and situations portrayed are fictitious and are not based on actual places
or persons whether living or dead.

All rights reserved. No part of this publication may be reproduced,
stored in a retrieval system, or transmitted in any form or by any means,
electronic, mechanical, photocopying, recording or otherwise,
without prior permission of the copyright holder.

ISBN 978-1-906236-27-4

British Library Cataloguing in Publication Data
A CIP catalogue record for this book is available from the British Library

Set in Goudy Old Style by SilverWood Books
Printed in England on FSC paper by CPod, part of the Cromwell Press Group

# On Calico Wings

*by*

Jan Hedger

*Dedication*

This book is dedicated to my husband Nigel,
for the contentment within me,
and the love he has brought into my life.

## Thanks

Heartfelt thanks go to Flow for All (Forces Poetry)
through whom I have learned so much.
Many thanks go to Shorelink Community Writers,
with thanks also to GROW.

*Be Blessed as you Travel the Journey*

*Jan Hodge xx*

# Foreword

*On Calico Wings*, the title of this long awaited second book by Jan Hedger, develops beyond the content of her first book *Words in Imagination*.

The author's writing includes many aspects of life today, and shares comparisons with the past, showing great sympathy with all her subjects. Her nature poems contain word pictures to compare with the great poets of the past, yet remain true to today's way of life.

Gentle humour, love of music, coupled with real empathy and understanding for those affected by war, military personal, their families and friends, reaching out to all who read her work.

*On Calico Wings* is a book which contains poems deserving, like all good poetry, to be performed to a live audience and the author often does this. However, this book can equally be enjoyed as a travelling companion, to be opened and pondered upon, on the journey through life.

A R Lewis
2009

*Love, Life And Loss...*

# Calico

Alone on the bench
she sat watching

Calico, on a
shimmering sea
drifting, drifting
sailing the breeze
lazily billowing
catching the air
harnessing
its power
quite naturally
In quiet contemplation
she dreams, of being

Calico
adrift and free
amidst the
dancing sunlight
of her own
reflection, to
feel the breeze
revelling in all
its serenity

Silently, she entered
a darker world of

Calico drowning
in salty tears
unable to breathe
suffocating, despair
dragging her
down, down
as the storm
releases its power
destructively

Grasping for hope
she reaches out

And sails now
on calico wings
peacefully
drifting in the
pure clean air
above the
shimmering sea
remembering
quite reflectively

A girl sitting
alone on a bench
wishing…

## Waves Of Emotion

The sea appears ghostlike
From under the blanket of mist
Its waves gently rising
Gently falling, until…
It stealthily reaches the shore
Encroaching; Encompassing;
Possessing all within its grasp
Until… At the turn of the tide
It leaves as ghostly and
As gently as it came.

The sea rages forth
Beneath the stormy clouds
Its waves violently crashing
Violently pounding, until…
It throws itself on to the shore
Forcefully; Fiercely;
Powerful in its intent
Until… At the turn of the tide
Against its will, it retreats
Its mighty force spent.

The sea mirrors the blue sky
In the reflection of the baking sun
With hardly a wave at all
It lazily, seductively laps
At the foot of the golden shore
Luxuriantly; Lusciously;
Romantic in its embrace
Until… At the turn of the tide
It yields to its master's call
And the spell is broken.

## *Tides Of Change*

Barefoot on the sands
Holding hands
Eyes gazing into,
Each other's soul
That holds,
The love within
Hearts racing
All embracing
Two as one.

Now as one
She stands alone
Withdrawn,
Into her lonely soul
That holds,
The hurt within
Waves breaking
Heart aching
At love's demise.

# The Sea... Is A Cauldron

Out of the turbulent blackness
Surges forth molten grey steel
Spewing out its anger
Upon the darkened shore.
The midnight sea is raging
Fuelled by a gale force wind
The rain it is a-lashing down
Depression; it descends.

## *Ravaged By Love*

I am in Eden – and the steamy silence is broken,
by the freeing from my mind of tropical birds;
beautiful iridescent birds – that were caught,
in my imagination – are now at liberty,
amongst the palms and I relish them.
They call out their joy – their singing,
awakens my senses – and I dance!
My cool muslin dress floats about my ankles
and I am weightless
I whirl around, and around –
lost in my world – I hadn't noticed,
the re-emergence of silence.
My hands fly up to protect my head,
from hundreds of birds –
falling dead – around me – and,
I am running through a carpet of feathers,
no longer soft – but sharp and cutting my feet.
The intricate weave of my fabric – is now,
blood red – it is spoilt – I rip it from my body
exposing my naked flesh –
it is the last humiliation.
I jump – and the glass shatters around me,
forming an ocean at my feet – with
the moonlight dancing on my bareness –
I step into its reflection – and am,
Swallowed – by its warm salinity.

# The Arrangement

His fingers caught in the tresses of her hair,
As he whirled her – high in the dance.
His dark, deep set eyes held possessiveness.
The intensity of her eyes flashed defiance.
He would not be denied;
She would not be promised.
As the music lifted, his arm
Tightened around her belted waist,
Slender – against the breadth of him.
The light from the all-consuming fire
Reflected lambent upon her wilful face,
But it did not diffuse the anger there.
Dust swirled in the charged air as the beat
Intensified its pace; the notes hypnotic
The deftness of their feet tracing a path
Of pre-determined destiny.
Palm to palm, the onlookers encircled the pair,
Knowledge and tradition uniting their eyes,
In the taming of the child.
The strings of the fiddle pulsated
In response to the travelling bow
Enrapturing, capturing the girl with its spell.
As the sweat emerged in silver beads,
Upon his brow, he pulled her in
To the aroma of his manly scent.
Intoxicating her senses, quickening the blood
That flowed through the chambers of her heart;
Infusing her cheeks with a blush of softness.
His rough hands – instinctual – felt the burning passion,
That mirrored his body's own needs and desires.

Detecting the change, he halted in his step,
And met the full force of a woman's eyes.
Coquettish – she loosened the red cotton twill
He wore knotted about his neck – tantalisingly,
Feeling its coarseness – running through her,
Soft velvety fingertips. She was his.
The music slowed – became still – as the evening's breath.
In one body, the onlookers retreated to their beds;
Consigning the embers to shift and settle in the dying fire.

# Just A Trace
*(Villanelle)*

The way the sun fell on your face
A dent in the pillow still nestles there
Your sweet perfume, now just a trace.

When we first kissed, in that distant place
I loved you then my heart lay bare
The way the sun fell on your face.

My emotions caught as fine as lace
Fingers entwined in your silky hair
Your sweet perfume, now just a trace.

You came to me in given grace
Ready for our love to share
The way the sun fell on your face.

But your soul, I could not encase
No commitment, would you declare
Your sweet perfume, now just a trace.

The night melted, we held embrace
Glowing; in the morning air
The way the sun fell on your face
Your sweet perfume, now just a trace.

## Her Love

He roused her from deep hibernation
With his warm, soft sensual kisses
His gentle hands caressing, exploring…

Beads of perspiration formed
On their freshly bathed bodies
In the sultry air, of an early summers night.

Responding, she nuzzled into his neck
Taking in the scent of him, the taste of him
As her sweet lips moved over his body, exciting…

And deep into the night, she loved him.

## Her Wedding

On the eve of her wedding, she reflected,
but did not step back
On the morn of her wedding; she knew who she truly was
At the time of her wedding, she walked forward, and
placed her trust in his love.

## *Wedding Dress Shopping*

Softly flowing in a cascade of Ivory white
Blossoming in a wedding gown
A bodice in the contour of her
Fitting perfectly, then flatteringly,
Falling into a pool at her feet
Eyes meet in a moment of clarity,
This is the one.

## A Secret Shared

A secret told to earnest ears
Striving to catch, each,
Whispered word
Eyes wide open in surprise
Breath – drawn in and held
To be exhaled in a tumble
Of excitement
Through cupped hands
Shielding a receptive ear.
And so it goes on
Until the secret
Is no longer; secret.

## Lies Told

Words flow like a waterfall
A tumbling tissue of lies
Spoken to ears, that only,
Hear what they want to hear
Gathering into pools
In the subconscious mind
Overflowing, into a,
River of thought.
Clarity dawns
And the lies are,
Discovered, uncovered
And denounced.

# *Exposed*

I do not need to,
Strip you naked
You did that yourself.
I don't need your finery
For even in jeans
I'm at ease with myself.
Silk does not a person make
Nor rags define a tramp.
It's in our inner selves,
Where the truth lies
And your lies,
Expose the truth.

## Still Life

The bruised red velvet
petals of the three red roses
curl in tight, in solidarity, against
the invasion of their inner selves.
Not so the brazen lily, who bares her soul
her fiery orange tongue; resplendent.
Soft, pink lacy fingers of the
unassuming astilbe
reach out to them, in harmony.
All hold their breath; lie still
on the crisp white linen.
Click; click the only sound.
With a long gentle sigh
they relax; knowing their life
is recorded for ever.

## *Friends; Always*

She sent me a feather
From her gossamer wings
Knowing I needed comfort
Belief and her support
As always

My heart skipped a beat
As I picked up the feather
And held it soft in my hand
As I will hold the memory of her
With me, always

Such a gentle feather
Like the gentlest of smiles
That adorned her pretty face
I'll smile with you, and
For you, always

I imagine the feather
Dipped in paint of purest blue
Bringing life to a blank canvas
At the touch of her hand
An artist, always

A pure white downy feather
From the breast of a bird
Flying free in the sky
The wonder of nature loved by her
And by me, always

This feather brings these words
A tribute to her faith
In me and in my poetry
Amanda, my inspiration
Always

## *Absence*

The paint swept across the easel
Frenetic, wild, and out of control
Imagining a canvas there...
There being none;
Its tears fell to the floor
Pooling into a cascade of colour
On the cold, stone tiles
Of the deserted artist's studio

# *Seashell*

My shell is my home
        but without table and chairs
Just a cool empty space
        in which to lay my head
Do I get pleasure from being
        afloat in the salty sea?
Do I gleefully scoff as I escape
        the trawler man's nets?
Do I get a thrill from being the first
        in the race to reach the shore?
Do I find comfort in clinging
        steadfastly to the rocks?
Do I feel sorrow or sadness
        at the end of my life?

No, I feel deep joy at the
        squeal of delight
Of a girl in a pink summers dress
        as she picks up the shell
Off the beach, from where
        I left it behind.

## *Innocent Grief*

I wanted to play
But you'd gone away
Mommy was crying
Grandma was sighing
'What will you do
Now you are two?'
I held mommy's hand
Tried to understand
Why she was sad
And where was my dad?
She patted my head
Said 'go back to bed'
Gave me a smile
'I'll be up in a while'
I climbed the stairs
Knelt for my prayers
Dear God in the sky
Do you know why
When I wanted to play
You took him away.

*Dreaming*

I miss my dreams
Now my sleep is poor
They were my escape
From reality
Now reality has won
It keeps me awake
Shattering my dreams
My illusions of life
I miss my dreams.

I make my bed in the morning
And tuck my dreams up tight
Promising them that I'll return
Once more when it is night!

A sea of dreams
awash with hope
surfing the waves
of one's ambition.

A dream
To reach
A dream
To achieve
Is there
Within your grasp
If you believe
You'll reach
Your dream
Your dream
You will achieve.

She dreams…
And lost herself in his kisses
Came alive in his embrace
Shivered at his gentle touch
As in one fleeting moment
A thousand butterflies
Came alive, and
Fluttered through her body
And found nowhere to land
Within her sleeping form.

A dream is an escape from the humdrum of life
From the nine to five, to rotational shifts
From shopping, ironing and washing the floor
A dream can give your heart a lift
Like a good cup of tea, or freshly brewed coffee
A slice of rich chocolate cake, all gooey!
So indulge yourself, at least once a day
And let your dreams take you away!

There is no future in the past.
Memories of the mind
Cannot be recreated
For nothing is the same twice.

Look to dreams of the future
For that is where destiny lies.
Not in that what is left behind.
Turn the key; lock the door
Archive it.

Climb the mountain of hope
To reach your cloud of dreams

Traverse the clear blue sky
To tread your chosen path
Shoot as a shooting star
To aspire as to who to be
Do not fall as cold wet rain
That washes away your soul
But drift as pure white snow
Touching lives with your grace
Then shine out as strong as the sun
A reflection upon yourself!

I dreamt I saw an angel
Dressed in pure white lace
Her wings they did a flutter
As she beckoned from above
I wanted now to join her
To find freedom from the pain
But there was a hand that held me
From my man of forty year
I turned and met his tired eyes
And asked of him one last thing
My hand he then let slip away
You'll always be my angel, my friend.

*Emotions In Conflict...*

## *A Day To Remember*

As the poppy petals fall
It is then I recall
A winters November eve
Cosy and warm, with my mom
In front of the tele
Watching the Remembrance service
From the grand Albert Hall
It was important, she said,
To remember.
I didn't understand then
Just knew my heart felt strange
As I watched the soldiers parade.
Then it was up early next morn
To go to my aunt's
In Stechford, a bus ride away
To stand at the Cenotaph
Wrapped in scarves, the family together
It was important, they said,
To remember.
I didn't understand then
Just knew my heart felt strange
As I watched the soldiers parade.
Ever since then as I have grown older
I have always put aside that date in November
I understand now, why it's important to remember
And it is pride that I feel in my heart
As I watch the soldiers parade.

# No Goodbye For A Mother

With purity of innocence
they stand in white
row upon row
on the restful green.
Silver dewdrops cling
to shortened
blades of grass
afraid to let go.
The crimson
of spilt blood
washes away into
the pink of dawn.
All that remained
from the black night
was wrapped tightly
round the kneeling woman.
All that remained
from the scarlet red
was in the poppy she wore.
For death is final
in its leaving.
It is the grieving
that lives on,
in the breathing.

*Footnote: a war cemetery across the water;
a death without a goodbye.*

'Shot at Dawn' was the phase given to the execution of those labelled as cowards on the battlefields of World War One. These brave young men were not cowards, they were suffering the devastating effects of shellshock – now known to be PTSD. Some were no more than boys, thrust into the horror of trench warfare. Amidst the mud, the pain and the daily sight of death, these young minds were emotionally shattered.

Often used an example, as a warning to others and with an illegal court martial, they were shot by their own unit, forced to make up the dawn firing squad.

Some could not live with their guilt.

After a relentless campaign by many committed to the cause, all 306 soldiers of the First World War that were shot at dawn for cowardice or desertion, have now been granted posthumous pardons.

# Too Young

Please Sir, don't make me do this
He's my mate, he's only young Sir
He broke the rules lad
And sentence is passed
Now come on soldier
Move along there
But, me legs won't move Sir
I'm shaking, look
What are you soldier
Man or mouse?
I'm neither man nor mouse Sir
I am just a boy, a boy
Just like my brother Sir
Then aim true lad
And spare him pain
Soldier, cock that rifle
Or you'll find yourself
Against that wall
But, but Sir I can't see
I'm blinded Sir
Enough now soldier
Pull that trigger
And that my boy
IS AN ORDER!

CRACK!

I am sorry, so sorry mate…
Was the last cry he uttered
As he fell by the hand,
Of his own gun
Never to be a man.

## *Forget Them Not*

Forget me not he said to me
My love so pure and true
Forget me not sweet wood anemone
As I take my leave of you
For a soldier blue I am to be
And it's off to war I go
Across the wide and deep blue sea
To a land I do not know
Forget me not till I return
And save a place for me.

Oh my brave wee soldier blue
I whispered in soft reply
My love for you is also true
It will not fade and die
However long we are apart
And as I bid you fair adieu
I'll hold you fast within my heart
And weep with pride for you
Until the day that you return
And I'll save a place for you.

Now three long years and two have past
And my love's returned to me
Not as a blue forget me not
Instead, a poppy of tissue red
And this he had to say;

My sweet anemone, what I have done
Has ripped my very soul apart
I've slain with knife, I've killed with gun
And returned with a wounded heart
Bleeding for each mother's son
As the loaded dice was cast
And though the war was won
The price we paid was vast
So many who did not return
So many lives to mourn.
And you my sweet anemone
Do you love me still?
Is their a place for me?

Oh! I cried in sweet refrain
Though boy to man you've changed
My love for you as always been
I shall not desert you now
Come rest your head upon my breast
We will forget them not.

*The following extract is taken from 'A Moment in Time' by AR Lewis, written from personal experience during the evacuation of Dunkerque where, as a young soldier, he stood on watch overnight for incoming boats.*

I was one of those soldiers, and remember the strange feeling of a complete lull from all the noise, as though the whole World had been stilled. Then as I looked around me observing the ships on fire, the smoking Town behind me, the only sound that of the waves hissing and sighing at my feet, with bits of equipment, and dead bodies of Soldiers, and Seamen being gently washed ashore.

In that brief spell just before dawn when all is silent, and waiting that first burst of life. Amongst all that carnage of death and destruction, I suddenly realized I was looking at an incredible scene of indescribable beauty.

The effervescent sand sparkled with colour like a field of diamonds, with the movement of the ebb and flow of the tide all along the shore line. The bodies of the dead lying on the water's edge all edged with effervescence, as though encased in a sparkling Halo of reverence.

The quietness, the effervescence, the smoke and flames, all combined to give a feeling, that just for that brief time some unseen hand had created a picture of intense beauty, and I was left with the feeling that I was being privileged to experience something very special, even in that time of great stress.

Then suddenly a shout, as more boats appeared, the vision vanished, and the mayhem started again.

*Such a beautifully written, personal account deeply moved me and it inspired the following poem...*

# Dawn At Dunkerque
*(A Reflection)*

'Lives extinguished into darkness
And yet, ethereally luminescent'

Beauty from out of carnage
How can this possibly be
When the words themselves
Are the opposite ends of the scale
Is there a force we do not know
That exists in the air around us
A force that we choose to ignore
As it doesn't fit into the square box
We recognise as life's existence
A life granted to us alone
But it is a tenuous life, that
Can be so cruelly taken away
By setting man against man,
Upon the stage of warfare
Where it is only death,
That waits in the wings
And glory is not the final encore
For when the curtain rises
The tragedy begins again.

*The next poem is for all those who suffered, and those who lost their lives in the construction of the 'Hohlsgangsanlagen' – what we know today as The Jersey War Tunnels/Underground Hospital – during the German occupation of the Channel Islands.*

*Many were exiles, from The Spanish Civil War, who had fled to France – already low in moral from their own fight – they found themselves now as victims in another war. In their mind, hopes and dreams, they never lost sight of their true homeland and never gave up hope that one day they would return.*

## *Absolution*

My fingers are torn and bleeding
My skin has shrunk to my bones
I have no strength, such is my hunger
Starvation is cruel and unyielding
And the cold, always the cold
Their is no heat here in Ho8
'The tunnels below the earth'.
I swing my pick axe, and a
Small piece of rock falls at my feet
It is not enough; they are angry
The blows from their sticks
Fall upon my shoulders
I tell myself I am immune!
But I am not, and it hurts
I feel unbearable pain
Would my mama recognise me now?
The once proud son she bore?
I think not; I cry out for her
Mama, mama! And they beat me once more.
Close by an explosion echoes
Showering us in red sandstone dust
Now we are not so different
Brothers; eyes locked in fear
For they have a mama too.
The heavy sound of footsteps
Cuts into the moment; they are panicking
I am hauled to my feet
And forced to join the slow moving ranks
Of the lost souls of men
Slaves of the German Third Reich

Leaving their dead behind.
The passage is long and the way unstable
An old man slips and falls
Amongst the polished boots
Desperately his fingers clasp my ankle
He calls to me 'Comrade, I beg of you'
I ignore him and shake him free
In my single-mindedness to reach the light.
Oh! Such bitter sweet relief
To taste the sweet, sweet air
I close my eyes and am lost in its freedom
My mind elsewhere; I see papa!
Working the land of my birth
But no; it is the old man that is there!
Oh my papa! My papa! Forgive me!
I couldn't help him! Dear God, I couldn't help him!
And as the evening sky descends upon me
I fall to my knees in repentance
My darkness is absolute.

# Hey, I Feel Pain Too!

Why do you assault me?
I have been here for millions of years
Solid, whole and unyielding.
I shake with my anger at your invasion
And cover your bodies in my sandstone dust.
You have joined me now,
Here for ever.

*Footnote: 'Thinking out of the box'.*
*Whilst writing 'Absolution' I got to thinking how the 'rock' felt. People are not the only victims of war, as we see in the next poem.*

## *Belonging*

Oh, I am having such a wonderful time!
This war brings new life; warmth into my cold walls
When I hear that long drawn out sound
I know they are coming!
Families; children, mothers and fathers
The smell of kitchens, floor-polish, nurturing me
Comforting, wrapping their arms around me
Saying 'we are here, you are loved!'
I enfold them in my space
Protecting them; it is my job.
I have shared the brief kiss of a departing lover
Watched babes suckle, as the matriarchal mother,
Tells stories of hope to sleepy-eyed children, whilst,
The quiet tears of her grief intermingle with mine.
I have felt every frustrated footstep
of a pacing father
Saying 'I shouldn't be here!'
I want to tell them 'I am here!'
But I have not been granted the power of speech
Instead I am the silent presence
Who they run to in their fear
But, what about me? What about my fear?
Oh! Let it never end – don't lock me away
Alone once more
Life was so lonely for a cellar
Before the bombs came.

## *Enduring Love*

Love, blossomed pink
   on the fair skin
of the sweet lass
   awaiting;
The young man, late
   rushes in haste
the violets crushed
   in his hand;
Arm in arm
   they strolled
along the promenade;
   The girl
and her soldier
   Precious times
together; in 1939.

A broad smile, beamed
   from the woman
with a ring of violets
   in her hair;
The weary soldier
   steps down
from the train
   returning her wave;
Meeting eyes
   they embraced
oblivious to the crowd;
   The bride to be
and her groom
A future life
   to live together; in 1945.

## *Here Lies*

War
Raw and Bloody
Lives lost
Selflessly in honour
Medals awarded
Telegrams delivered
Mothers crying
Wives weeping
Fathers grieving
Children,
Not understanding
Just seeing flags
Glory, and
Planes overhead.

But war is not glory
War; is names,
Carved for eternity;
Onto cold hard stone

## *In The Light Of*

Barbed wire on the beaches
Shrapnel in the streets
Blackout curtains at the windows
Keeping in the light.

Down the air raid shelter
Huddled under the stairs
Hiding like rats in a cellar
A candle for a light.

A screaming sound then silence
The bomb exerts its force
Destroying an entire street
In one flash of light.

The A.R.P. stands watching
Alert and on patrol
For a second they do nothing
Blinded by the light.

With calloused hands they dug
To free the injured folk
As firemen aimed there hoses high
To douse the blazing light.

Many didn't make it
And many tears were shed
Prayers were said to guide them
In God's eternal light.

Upon the news of the surrender
Fireworks lit the sky
Bonfires burned and beacons blazed
In defiant light.

No air raid warning sounded
Folk slept safe in bed
And new horizons beckoned
With the dawning of the light.

# Side By Side – They Lie In Peace Now

Across the English sea
Lie the brave and true.

White granite as their duvet
Dark earth as their bed
They fell upon the field of war
No soft pillow; for their head.

Blanketed was the world
In its stricken grief
As the death toll rose and rose
Futures stolen; war its blatant thief.

*Footnote: lines written after a poignant visit to Wimereux Commonwealth War Graves Cemetery – where due to the nature of the sandy soil the headstones are laid flat upon the ground.*

# *A Bag Is For Life!*

A BAG IS FOR LIFE!
The posters scream
Meat, raw and bloody
Falls from re-used carriers
Thin with over use
Onto the wet car park.

A BAG IS FOR LIFE!
Buy one today!
Screams the sign
By the check out till
As it eats up the pounds
From overloaded trolleys.

A BAG IS FOR LIFE!
Made of sackcloth and ashes.
Why ashes? The remnants of life.
Because today, I saw,
Images of the Bosnian war,
Body upon body, upon body
Buried in plastic bags;
And I wanted to scream,
A BAG IS FOR LIFE!

*Footnote: this poem was inspired by images from the Bosnian war, taken by Giles Penfound.*

*The images I saw affected me deeply.*

## *In Whom Do I Trust?*

Me mate and me
out on patrol
eyes peeled
for any unrest,
scanning the roofs
for snipers.
A car cruises past
thumping hearts
till it speeds on by
danger imagined.
A rock – skirted
for fear it's real,
every step
a threat.
A typical day in Iraq.

Then in a vision
comes a woman
in black,
laden with goods
fresh from
the market.
Weighed down
she stumbles
dropping her wares.
Quick as a flash,
unrehearsed
my mate races –
across the dusty road.

I meet her look
stomach churning
something's not right
something is wrong
the body is old
but the eyes are young.

I scream
GET B-A-C-K!
as the
water melon
EXPLODES
in his hand –
into fragments
of man – woman
into pulp of
flesh and bone.

I rock myself
to sleep
that night
full of
questions
full of doubt.

TELL ME; how
can I defend
when I know not
who to trust?

TELL ME; how
can I fight
when I achieve no good?

TELL ME; how
can I fight
in a war that's unjust?

HOW can I kill
a woman
in cold blood?

TELL ME;
Anybody!
Somebody,
Answer me.

For I do not know
I just don't know anymore
I just don't know.

*Footnote: inspired after hearing a poem – written by Brian Turner (War Poet) – which he read out on Poetry from the Front Line on Radio 4 – where the women and children you befriend one day could 'dance on your grave tomorrow.'*

## Left On The Train

Another soldier died today
Relegated to page seven
Behind the tabloid news of
'Crack' celebrities, and
Footballers cheating on their wives
He deserved better than that
Another soldier died today
Another family grieves.

*Footnote: I wrote this after picking up a discarded newspaper off the train, and was disturbed that the death of a soldier was indeed on page seven.*

## *Empty Teacups*

The knock came at night, crashing into the midnight stillness.
Pulling the bedclothes high, I encased myself in their security
Abject fear engulfing every muscle, every sinew in my body.
Dad was the one who moved, sliding bare feet into slippers
As if they were placed there in position for this very reason.
I felt his cold, tremulous hand, gently rest upon my shoulder
Just briefly; before the incessant knock sounded again.
As he clicked the bedroom door quietly, but firmly behind him
I felt an overwhelming vacuum of complete and utter emptiness
The blood draining from my heart, leaving in its wake an echoing beat
I buried down deeper, to silence it. I am sorry Dad, you have to go alone.
I willed myself, indeed ordered myself to return to the state of sleep
To hide, from the compelling, waiting truth, behind tightly shut eyes
See the nightmare through, wake up refreshed, to a new spring day.
A day renewed with hope, that in two weeks my boy WILL be home!
Two weeks is nothing, for I waited twenty years for him to be born

There came no others; he is my one pride and joy; and still my baby.
I don't know if I did sleep, or just lay comatose into the early hours
But daylight was filtering through the curtains when my head obeyed,
A sudden, inexplicit need to lift itself from the pillow comfort.
I thrust my arms firmly into the sleeves of a blue, corded dressing gown,
With a belied resoluteness, that I should pull myself together, be strong,
Go down, put the kettle on, Dad will need a cup of tea, sweet tea, always a comfort in a crisis, it's what they had drunk in the other war.
My tread fell soft upon the carpeted stair, tentative and afraid,
Of the hidden truth of realisation, that awaited me; for a mother knew.
Dad was standing looking out at the garden, where a swing once stood
His shoulders stooped, his body collapsed, barely holding the weight of his frame
Lost in his own pain, he didn't hear me come in, or feel my presence in the room.
It was the teacups that did it; just three white empty teacups,
Drained by the midnight callers, leaving their mark on the polished table.

A scream I couldn't suppress unleashed itself from the depths of my womb
Filling the air with a grief that would never be explained or understood.
'It's our boy, isn't it Dad. It's our boy, he's gone. My baby's gone'.
Dad caught me just before I fell, 'I know mom' he uttered with a strangled sob, 'I know'.

# Seasons Change – But War Remains

A verdant summer
Camouflage of soldiers
In a jungle war
Green leaves fall
And turn to dust
The dust of a soldier
In a desert war.

## *The Memorial*
### Bexhill On Sea 09/11/2008

Down at the promenade on Remembrance Sunday
For the open air service of thoughts and prayers
The English Channel, a reminder, a memory,
For many; for me – a sea of history.
And in my thoughts, I ask curiously…

Does the sea know, it saved us from the invading footfall
Does it know it carried men to war and boys to serve
Does it know it rescued the trapped from Dunkerque
And does it know that its storms drowned others.

Does the sea know, it swallowed planes whole
Does it know submarines lurked in its depth
Does it know that mines floated on its buoyancy
And does it know, they wrecked many a ship.

Does it know, that it brought the boys home
Does it know they shed salty tears in its wake
Does it know a welcome lined its English shore
And does it know a people's gratitude.

Hark, speaks the whistling wind
The answer you seek is yes
For the sea and I are united
In our remembrance of the past.
With all the wreaths in place
I turned for home, content;
That the sea, the wind and I,
Had shown our joint respect.

form
# A Mix Of Emotions...

# He's Just One

A New York Street after the rain
yellow cabs swishing as they
take the bejewelled and bedecked
home to suburbia.

Steam issuing in a hiss from
the grid iron drains
resonates a silent sound
which permeates the damp air.

The heckler staggers home
his words slurred
no rhythm or rhyme
at all in his life.

Head down, he turns his
frayed collar up against the
creeping dankness.

Neon lights flicker
in rainbow reflection
a contrast to his
monochrome existence.
and for a moment
he hesitates –
before descending the
cracked concrete steps
to his one-roomed
basement apartment.

## Bottle Alley

They hide from the sun
They hide from themselves
They hide in a bottle
In denial
Who stole their lives?
In Bottle Alley
With shattered glass
Of shattered lives
They sit.

*Footnote: Bottle Alley is an area of St Leonards, where vagrant alcoholics used to congregate. It takes its name from pieces of coloured glass decoratively inserted into its back wall. I make no apologies for its inclusion in this book; as quoted by Tom O'Brien writer of the play 'Down Bottle Alley' (adapted from the book 'My Wretched Alcoholism: This Damned Puppeteer' by Brian Charles Harding) – 'there are similar places – and similar people – in every town'.*

# *Untitled*

He died alone in a furnished room
A crumpled duvet lay cold upon his form
In the kitchen, an inherent reminder of a simple,
Last unhurried meal, microwaved for one
Grains of rice, defying removal remain their still
Shelf upon shelf of escapism from reality
James Bond 007 ejected in the video
Is this who aspired to be in his mind?
Did he imagine a woman bathed in gold was his?
I'd like to think so.
A few possessions lay scattered
An old photograph, no frame; treasured.
They stood in this furnished room and paid their last respects. There were those who cared.

## *Injustice*

Men of the city of London
Eat Marks and Spencer sandwiches
Visit the local sushi bar
And drink cool chardonnay
Under a striped parasol
Of a trendy street café.

The homeless boys of London
Eat scraps from litter bins
A crust and half a sausage roll
A can of cheap cider, quenching
An ever growing thirst
In the heat of a July day.

Men of the city of London
Go home to four bedroomed houses
Nestled in the Kent countryside
Home to their socialite wives
And four course dinner parties
Cigars and glasses of wine.

The homeless boys of London
They have nowhere to go.
Just a doorway as their haven
And a cardboard box or two
A sleeping bag wrapped round them
Alone they beg for food.

## *Reclamation*

They call this a pass, a pass to where?
When there is no door, for the ones issued in orange
I was too old for a blue, too young for a green
And not disabled in body for a yellow.
The twenty to thirty year-olds, they said
Were strong, needed to stay and defend.
Defend what? All that is left,
Is dusty scrubland,
After the comet came.
It came at night, caught us unawares
A technical hitch, in the technology, they said
A computer glitch.
Well that's what happens
When you employ monkeys.

I said at the time
It wouldn't work.
Now all I have is a pass,
A pass to nowhere
Whilst the monkeys; go deluxe
First class
My world is theirs,
To reclaim at last.

## A Nurse Abroad

The mirror showed a reflection
of a woman in her prime
forty years behind her
knowledge in her eyes

She'd seen the world
travelled far and wide
had cried with joy
celebrated life

Mourned lost friends
cried with grief
known love and hate
been a rock

Sun-bleached hair
framed her face
an image
of compassion

She'd found faith
when it was lost
had given hope
when there was none

Asked for nothing
in return
to have been there
was enough

Felt proud
was humbled
to be honoured
in this way

A touch of lipstick
a nervous smile
her thoughts collected
she was ready

'We are gathered
here today
to reward
a dear friend,
for her loyalty
and humanity
through war
and in famine,
Ladies and Gentlemen
I give you
a remarkable woman.'

*A poem for all nurses and carers throughout the world, for their diligence, commitment and humanity.*
*All are remarkable people.*

# *The Unused Room*

Speckled dust, dances on the mahogany table
Flecked particles perform acrobatics in the stale air
Caught in the footlights of the afternoon sun
They perform for no one, but themselves.

Closed books, bound in secret line one wall
Two portraits hang opposite, seeing only each other
No one else to say goodnight too, or God bless
The bed linen folded pristine, cotton creases sharp.

Spiders seek refuge in the darkened corners
Scurrying away from the searing brightness
Surging its way through the leaded windows
Into a waterfall of light, on the bare wooden floor.

Few home comforts remain in this modest room
Perfume, long since evaporated and a silk gown
Are in themselves just hints that a woman slept here
An authoress who penned her work, undisclosed.

People talk of her now, read her stories of romance
Adapt her works for film and television audiences
The historic family home preserved by English Heritage
A blue plaque sited by the solid front door.

The room itself remains virtually untouched
Sacrosanct to her memory
And her life.

# Grass

I feel the silkiness of its
fleeting touch upon my
bare exposed feet.
My linen skirt swishing
around my ankles
just teasingly
brushing its surface.
A straw hat is perched
upon my auburn hair
a living connection
to the earth.
I place my chequered rug
(as it invited me to do)
upon its textured skin
creating a perfect square
of intimate darkness.
Folding myself into its
sweet scented fragrance
I allow it to become
part of me, a channel
for my thoughts.
Taking out my pen
and trusty notebook
I begin to write…

Grass

I feel the silkiness …

*Inspiration...*

## *Flower Of The Mountain*

I would grow beside the cool crystal water
To bear witness to the birth of its being
With its orchestration of musical sound
Pure and sweet in its joy of living
Tumbling and twisting and rushing to be
A winding river that leads to the sea

I would unfurl mine eye to meet the sun
And there in its light an eagle is soaring
With powerful ease and beauty sublime
Bronzed and golden wings far-reaching
Rising and falling and proud to be
Untamed, unfettered and wild like me

For the flower I'd be, is the person I am
A seasoned survivor through adversity
With delicate strength of gentian blue
Uncomplicated in my simplicity
Alone, but oh; never lonely am I
In such beauty, at one with the sky

## *Tranquillity*

Oh dear sweet woodland of pure tranquillity
Oh how I bathe in your ethereal beauty
Nature's cathedral in majestic splendour,
Rising, aspiring, and saluting the sky.
Let not its silence fool you, nor its stillness belie
For if you pause a moment upon your passing through
You'll hear a choir of angels' song to freshen you anew.
All manner of creatures are there, although hidden
They'll bid you come! Come join in our congregation.
Do as they bid, my friend, and linger a while longer
Your heart will be lifted, your senses heightened,
Your resolve stronger.
Reach out; capture its essence secrete it away in your mind
So when you feel bruised and battered,
By the injustice of mankind
Release it; and let the scene unfold
Allow it to breathe; it's yours to behold.
Oh dear sweet woodland of pure tranquillity
Oh how I bathe in your ethereal beauty.

## *Poppies*

They come briefly, once a year
To grace our fields with delicate flair
Bursting forth in red aplomb
Peaceful, and yet all aflame
In celebration and remembrance;
I catch my breath as I espy
Upon my walk, a sea of poppies
Regale mine eye.

## *By the Brook*

Beside the babbling brook lay I
Ears cocked to hear his cry
Then I heard it, keen and long
The dog fox answer, my mating song
From yonder field beyond the glen
He answered thrice, I chose him then
For it was time.

Beside the babbling brook lay we
Content within our company
He'll not bide long, this I know
When twilight falls he will go
Whilst I retreat, below the earth
To await, the impending birth
For it is time.

Beside the babbling brook they play
This eve of Midsummer's day
 Pouncing, fighting, honing their skills
For survival is a battle of wills
A misty dawn, creeps o'er the hill
Dewdrops glisten and the land lies still
Staying strong, I ignore their cries
I have to break a mother's ties
For it is time.

Beside the babbling brook lay I
Ears cocked, to hear his cry
Then I heard it, keen and long
The dog fox answer, my mating song …

# Nature's Library

Mother Nature surrounds us in all her glory
No author could write such a wondrous story
A Mills and Boon romance
Swans' necks entwined on a shimmering lake
A mystical tale
Of snakes swaying, hypnotically staring
A mystery thriller
Whose footprints break the virgin snow?
A comedy of errors
Of skittish lambs, leaping and bleating
A children's fantasy
Of eagles, of mountains and far off lands;
The story of life evolving
Is ever growing, ever revolving
The book unfolds
Leaves ever turning
New chapters beginning
Nature is an endless story.

# The River

Down below in the glittering moonlight
Flows the silver of the night
A power as the source of life
The river it never sleeps.

# A Passage To Spring
(Rondine)

Time marches on – left, right, left, right
Slow down, draw your breath, stand at ease
Allow the winter to decrease
Let the wind lose its bite.
As a soldier wins the fight
In praise; fall to your knees
Time marches on.

Life goes on; in despite,
Of weakened sun and chilling breeze
Take a leaf from the trees
Praise the light and grow
Time marches on.

## *Believe in Self Belief*
*(Rondel Prime)*

Take a risk and leave the shadows
With vibrant clothes that sing out loud
Be yourself in rhythmic echoes
Emerge with strength, discard the shroud.

Draw your breath as the music grows
Play your cards, to the captive crowd
Take a risk and leave the shadows
With vibrant clothes that sing out loud.

Hail! The gift of melodic vows
With which we are richly endowed
Blow the whistle silvery proud
Hear the applause, embrace the bows
Take a risk and leave the shadows
With vibrant clothes that sing out loud.

## In The Wake Of Reflection

The sun broke through the clouds, shining its light upon the puddles, left by the downpour of rain. At one, a woman stood, looking down on her reflection. It scared her, frightened her, and disturbed her; where had the girl gone? Her innocence sullied and spoilt by him.
Shaking the droplets from her umbrella, she snapped it shut and stirred the water with its point, till it became muddy and unclear; as muddy and unclear as her mind felt at this present moment.
To the side of her, stood a greater body of water, a lake; calling her.
'Come into me and allow yourself to sink to my silted depths. Know life no more and free your mind from this burden you carry. Cleanse yourself in me.'
The woman moved closer to the edge. A second beam of light, stronger than the first, shone with such brilliance, it bought forth a rainbow.
She faltered, hesitated and instead of stepping into the water, she climbed onto and rode the rainbow; bringing colour back to her life.